men without h

Men Without I

MW00932526

A collection of poems
By
Diron Duah

men without hearts

from everything that i've touched
to everything that has touched me,
i'm thankful for either.

men without hearts

this is for everyone
who has had a
piece of my heart.

if you were brazen enough
to make memories with me
then you're in here somewhere.

an assembly of pain,
hurt,
disappointment,
heartbreak,
belief,
hope,
and love.

Poetry.

"After great pain, a formal feeling comes —."
-Emily Dickinson

men
without

hearts

men without hearts

why am i afraid to tell you who i am

i've given up trying to be yours
i'm trying to be mine again
that is what i miss

men without hearts

she's on fire
no wonder you called her burning beautiful
you only watched from a safe distance

how come you don't give up?

i wanted you to be the one for me so bad
that i rewrote the mixed signals
the reason i know you're the one is because
when you speak, i can smell the truth on your
breathe

suddenly,
it was never you
she was in love with
it was the idea of you

you gave the impression
that your love was a gift
i could not refuse

men without hearts

you sell me the idea that it's impossible
to be in two places at once
i guess you never watched me closely
i've been sad and happy
give me the credit i deserve

men without hearts

the trust and love i devoted to you
i wish i had done the same for my mother
for her love and trust fo me never waived
but mine was split between sharing it with you
and everyone else
now i know where my tears go

you were the first girl
i fell in love with
who showed me i could
be hugged ever so tightly
by a smile that grows arms
i miss that

.

leaving doesn't always mean gone
sometimes it means, please come find me

she never lost touch with her distasteful past
so don't offer her your unsavory future

she will come around and when she leaves you
you will be left pretending you're okay

men without hearts

are you hungry?

i've munched on the idea of love you fed me
my mind is full but my heart is empty

after everything ended,
i realized you keep stopping
in from time to time
to see how im doing
checking how things are going
with me and what's new
hopefully you're not wondering
if im doing better without you or
wanting to hear me crumble
just so you feel good
about your decision to leave
you wont see me fold

men without hearts

i don't have to self-inflict to hurt myself
all i have to do is think of you

i'm not mad you hurt me
i'm mad i let you hurt me

the end after the beginning

we got it right this time
we almost had it
we never had it

don't ask if she's in love with you
there's going to come a day
she'll look at you
in that gaze you'll
find the answer

men without hearts

from time to time
i'll borrow you into my dreams
just so i can fall back asleep
before morning comes

men without hearts

once upon a time
nothing was the same again
the end

for the fear of starting over
i'm left clinging to the reasons
why i still bleed for you

believe me,
i'm doing stuff for her
i never did for you but
i am still more in love with you than
i could ever be with her

i honestly thought
it was obvious
that i traded my
poetry for your
friendship and my need
for your attention

men without hearts

my cracks are not for you to fix
they are suppose to show you
all the places i have been
the hearts i've broken and
the ones yet to be broken

on my birthday you asked me to make a wish
blew out the candles on the cake
i wished under my breathe that i was in love with
you
i am not and i don't have the courage to tell you

wishes don't always come true

men without hearts

why do you look so tired?

let me tell you how much this love
i have for her has taken from me
let me tell you how much of myself
i've lost in the middle of all this chaos
let me show you all the scars i've incurred so far
honestly i'm not tired now
i have no more to give
i'm dying

men without hearts

men without hearts

the only time i mattered
was when your glass was full
so when you asked me if i loved you,
i asked , 'can i pour you some more?'

my fear of forever living in my past
engulfs my very being so much
that i'm forced to petition
the future to give me a glimpse
that what i'm yet to see
would be enough to make me forget
about all the wrong places i've been

if your heart will break,
you will hear it from a mile away
if your heart breaks,
at least you had one anyways

thanks for coming

you don't know what your love meant to me
so you had to break me to learn
that i will never be the same again
this was after i told you
hearts don't break around here
so i hope you got what you came for
knowing that i will never love again

men without hearts

no, no, no! i promise this has nothing to do with
you
see, before you there was another
honestly, before you there have been others
who came along and got pieces of me
and i swear when i found you,
you were the one i wanted to give my heart to
but if you can tell i would have had a hard time
getting all my pieces together
just to give you the heart you deserve
so please understand that somehow
this wasn't how i meant for it to happen
my heart just isn't mine anymore

the lies you told
have shutdown
all the pores
in your face
so sadly you
don't glow anymore

your name tastes like
a mistake i'm trying to forget

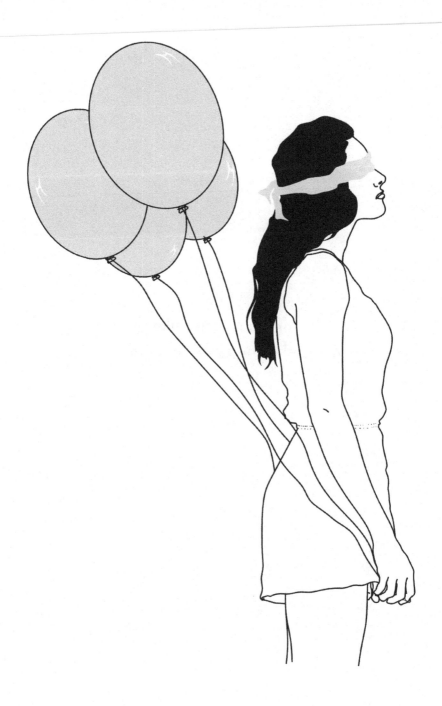

you collect hearts
you don't need
into jars
you won't keep

she's trying to stop lying to you
so please stop asking
her how she's doing
because she'll always for
the rest of time say she's okay
but you can tell from the look in her eyes
she's withering as fast as the seasons change

where do my tears go?

you only listen better when i cry
i fail to cry so you fail to listen

i knew it was a fool's gold kind of love
i still fell for you anyways

look at me now

men without hearts

the moment i realize i'm enough
nothing will be the same

all i ask

you were afraid to be forgotten
so you stayed past the hurt and pain
let's be honest, the love is long gone
but i will remember you
you were the one
i told not to hurt me
you did
i guess that was me asking for too much

men without hearts

in an attempt to erase all the places
you touched just so i could move on,
i resort to taking longer showers
with the notion that the running water
will wash away your fingerprints
laying savagely on my skin

i have the knack to lose words
when i need them the most
i lost words when we first met
i lost them when we last met
that hurts more often that sometimes

i cant tell which was worse
missing you knowing you're gone
or when you were next to me

men without hearts

don't ask her if she's in love with you
there is going to come a day
she will look at you
and in that gaze
you will find the answer

even before i knew you
i knew you would become someone
i used to know someday this day

the guy you say is condescending
do you know his story
have you seen the monsters
he hides in his closet

i refuse to see where you wish to take me
until i know where you're going

men without hearts

you've never always loved me
you've never always wanted me
you've never even given
yourself the chance to know me
not until i learnt to mimic your every motion
like a cactus in a desert
you sucked every stretch of water you could get
just so you could stay alive
so i became a mirror of you and for you
you look at me and you see
what you wanted me to be
and not who and what i am
so now i know you love me
i know you want me
i know this is your chance to know me
only for me to watch you leave
and cleave to the you i've become
and somewhat wandering in all the
hurtful places searching for who I was

you said it has been over
truth is, it has been over for one person

i have a thing for a girl
she's not what i've always wanted
she's what i've never had
she's what i'll ever want
what i'll ever need

it isn't what you gave that hurt
it's what you could give but chose not to

men without hearts

i used to be sad before i met you
but for some reason my sadness
does not want to meet you again

if you knew my worth
would you give me your best
you did not know my worth
so you gave me your worst

men without hearts

when i poured my heart into you
some called it foolish
i called it love
the language long forgotten

truth is
people don't fall out of love
they give up on love

i know i'll be happy again
you just won't be the reason

when i said lets go hiding,
i didn't mean literally,
i meant that once in awhile
i get to be you and you get to be me
and maybe you could see
how much you mean to me

men without hearts

i've been out on this cliff before
with women who swore they could
teach me how to fly
so i jumped off while they peeked over
and watched me hit the bottom
from way up high

you wanted to try that trick
where you had me close my eyes
and count to three and when
i opened my eyes you would be gone
this time i won't close my eyes.
if you wish to disappear
you can leave on one

men without hearts

behind the pretty face and smiles
lay the reason why i said i love you
with my eyes closed
because with my eyes open
i'd see through your lies, eyes

men without hearts

trading places

you taught me how to lie
i taught you how to die while being alive

when i lose my voice and the words
to tell you how i feel about you
please use my eyes to guide
you back to my heart

i can taste the miles
of all the places you've been
and feel your footprints on my chest
whenever i listen to the music you play
repeatedly

men without hearts

my tolerance for pain dissolved
when the same mouth that
used to serenade me
hurt me

don't wonder what i'll do without you
because you'll be impressed

men without hearts

she walks away from you
and never looks back
don't be offended
she just didn't expect
you to still be there
no one ever stays she said

i dare you to fall in love
i dare you to fall in love
i said, i dare you to fall in love
with someone or something
i dare you not to guard your heart
i dare you to let yourself feel again
whether love or hurt
the heart you carry will break
let it break into another

men without hearts

you
found
a reason
to leave but
you found no
reason to stay

she wasn't taught
to fix things
she was raised
to replace things
that were broken
your heart was
just another thing

men without hearts

i showed you the scars
of my bleeding past
and the crumbs of
a heart i still carry
but you still went on
to break me some more

you
said you
won't hurt me
so i loved you
you hurt me yet
i still loved you
you left me and yet
i'm still in love with you

men without hearts

my trust for you
fell as fast as the
leaves in the fall
i have no intention
of picking you up ever again

every part of me
has been pretending
to be doing just fine
since you've been gone
except my heart
it still yearns for you

for-never

i remember you asked
me not to hurt you
i told you i would hurt you
but not by breaking your heart
i'll hurt you by holding you
ever so tightly and never let go
you left, i stayed

in ti ma cy

/ˈin(t)əməsē/

noun

into me see

i still yearn for the me before you
as if the me after you is not enough

look what i've become of you

your looks got me
you were good to me
you looked good on me
you were not good for me

the difference

hidden talents

i don't always mean what i say
i don't say what i mean either
i smile when i think of her
i can't tell who will hurt me
i use like instead of love
i'm scared of commitment
i like tattoos
i pretend not to have fears
i pretend i don't like you
i casually cry
i die on the inside

the
only time
i say your name
will be the only
time i'm asked why
i'm less interested in love

men without hearts

you
called me
strong because
i nursed a wound
you couldn't see

you
ask me to say
what's on my mind
i say nothing because
my mind is empty
it's my heart that's full
and i know you
don't have a heart
for the heart of the matter

men without hearts

honey,
i let myself go
and allowed you
to tame me
into your beauty
but make sure
to feed me
when you make
a beast out of me

i can't tell which was worse
missing you now that you're gone or
when you were next to me

men without hearts

the thing about the
pain i carry is that
it comes in uninvited
and stays past it's due time
and leaves when it wants to

your heart is made of ice
you melt away every time
my sun appear

i thought me caring for you
would take some worry off
  your shoulders so that
you could care for me too

men without hearts

since you're gone,
do me a favor
stay gone

maybe
one day we can smell the air
just you and i
with our eyes closed
maybe
we will get
our lives back

because of this
broken heart that i carry
anytime i speak
everything comes out in pieces

you see me unlike you
when i say i'm going home
i'm coming to you
before you left
and never came back
you said you
were going home
i hope you made it

men without hearts

you gave the impression
that your love was a gift
i could not refuse
but i watched you leave with it

if you knew
i was not in love with you
as much as you were with me
would you still love me

men without hearts

i wont say i know everything about you
but i'll take this part of you and treat
it like the maze to your heart
on nights when you refuse to spill
the secrets of your broken heart
i stay up and watch you
maneuver in your dreams
just so i could catch a glimpse
of what you hold dear to your heart
that way i can sit in the same pool of
emotional truths and sulk in like a far cry
to all the culprits of all my battle scars
but my fear subsides when i realize
that i have dreams too
i just keep them in the same
dresser drawer i keep my pride
i don't always open it until
i need to show off a part of me to you
just so i can grow closer to you than ever

men without hearts

men without hearts

you and i
were never
meant to last

Made in the USA
Monee, IL
08 February 2021